Why Don't Listen

...and can only do
one thing at a time

**Lessons women need
to know about men**

Allan & Barbara Pease
PEASE TRAINING INTERNATIONAL

© Allan Pease 1999 All rights reserved.

First published by Pease Training International Pty. Ltd.
P.O. Box 12, Mona Vale. N.S.W. 2103. Australia.
Tel. (02) 99799000 Fax 99799099
Email peasetraining@compuserve.com
Web www.peasetraining.com

National Library of Australia
Pease, Allan & Barbara
Why men don't listen & can only do one thing at a time.
Communication (Psychology) 158'2
ISBN 0 9593 6585 0

Edited by The Peases, Lisa Tierney, Penny Walters,
Daniel Le Roux, Diana Ritchie
Illustrations by John Hepworth
Concept by Barbara Pease
Cover Design by Luke Causby
Printed by Australian Print Group
Layout by Karen Stirling

Distributed by:
Australia and New Zealand: HarperCollins
United Kingdom: Orion Publishing
South Africa: Oxford University Press
SE Asia: Times Books

~ Introduction ~

Men and women are different. Not better or worse - but different.

Our objective in producing this mini-book is to help you, the reader, learn more about both yourself and the opposite sex so that your interaction and relationships can be more fulfilling, enjoyable and satisfying. It's full of commonsense advice and scientific facts that are both powerful and humorous.

We dedicate it to all the men and women who have ever sat up at 2am pulling their hair out as they plead with their partners, "But why don't you understand?" Relationships fail because men still don't understand why a woman can't be more like a man, and women expect their men to behave just like women do.

Enjoy!

Allan & Barbara Pease

~ Men's Emotions ~

Don't push men to admit their mistakes. A man won't admit mistakes because he thinks you won't love him. Explain to a man what the reality is - a woman will love him more.

A woman knows everything about her children. Men are vaguely aware of some short people also living in the house.

Men love practical gifts.
Buy him a lawnmower,
screwdriver or mini-television
set. Avoid socks, undies
and romantic cards.

Uptight men drink alcohol and
invade another country.
Uptight women eat chocolate
and invade shopping centres.

When discussing
problems with him, don't
make a man feel wrong.
In being wrong, a man
considers himself a failure.

Men hate criticism, that's
why they like to marry virgins.

Men climb on to their rock to solve problems – women who follow them get kicked off.

Stressed men become quiet.
A woman feels that this
silence means he doesn't
love her or that he's angry.
So just ignore it.

Men flick channels on the TV
to forget about problems.

Men have nicknames for each other such as Dickhead, Wanker, Numbskull and Useless. These names avoid any hint of intimacy.

When he moans, "Make me some chicken soup/ fresh orange juice/ get me a hot water bottle/ call the doctor and make sure my Will is in order!", it usually means he's got a slight head cold.

~ Male Brain Function ~

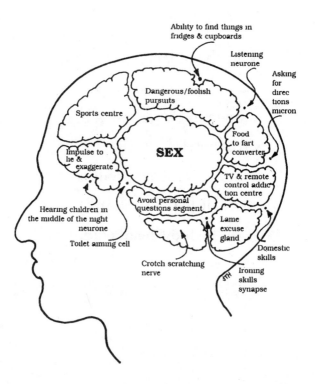

The Male Brain

Men's brains are
compartmentalised.
That's why they can
only concentrate on
one thing at a time.

If a man is shaving and you talk to him he'll cut himself. If he's hammering and the doorbell rings, he'll hit his thumb. If you talk to him when he's driving, he'll miss the turn-off. These are excellent revenge tactics.

The first rule of talking to
a man: Keep it simple!
Only give him one thing
at a time to think about.

When a man brushes his
teeth, his mono-tracked brain
focuses entirely on the task.
He stands square to the
basin, feet 30cms apart,
body bent over the sink,
moving his head back
and forth against the brush
to the speed of the water.

Choose his clothes for
important events. One
in every eight men is colour
blind to blue, red or green
and male brains have
limited ability to match
patterns and designs.
That's why it's easy to
spot a single man.

Men's brains miss the details.
When a man's brain is in a
resting state, scans reveal at
least 70% of its electrical
activity is shut down.

Men Miss The Details

Men prefer looks to brains
because most men can see
better than they can think.

Men have 'fix-it' brains.
When a man enters a room,
he scans it looking for
exits and entry points and
things that need fixing.

Men literally have 'tunnel vision'. That's why they're always so obvious when they look at other women. They have to turn their heads.

"We can't go on meeting like this, Goldie ... One day, Sam might take those blinkers off!!"

To get a man to listen, give him advance notice, a time limit and provide an agenda.

Having a mono-tracked brain
is why a man turns the radio
down to read a map or
navigate in heavy traffic.

Most men sleep better
when they are on the side of
the bed closest to the door.
This is the symbolic act of
defending the cave entrance.

Men use rest rooms
for biological reasons. No
man has ever been heard
to say, "Hey Frank, I'm
going to the toilet - you
wanna come with me?"

Men's eyesight is configured for long distances. That's why they can't locate things at close range — keys, socks, butter in the fridge, etc.

Men can't find things in fridges and cupboards

On long trips, men should drive at night and women drive during the day. A man's eyes see better into the distance at night than a woman's and men can tell which side of the road the oncoming traffic is on.

In a restaurant, let a man sit with his back to a wall, facing the restaurant entrance. This makes him feel comfortable, alert and in control.

To motivate a man to go shopping give him clear criteria – colours, sizes, brands, styles – tell him where you will shop and give a time limit.

A man can either read or listen - he can't do both

A man's concentration
is focussed. If a phone rings,
he will insist people stop
talking, music is turned
down and the TV is switched
off so he can answer it.

Men are poor at
differentiating sounds.
As a result, they don't
understand a woman's
phrase, "Don't use that
tone of voice with me!"
when arguing.

For a man, to talk is
to relate the facts.

Men see the telephone
as a communication
tool for relaying
information to other
people, and then
you hang it up.

A man speaks a daily average of around 7,000 communication 'words' to relate his message. This includes spoken words, voice changes and body language. A woman uses over 20,000.

Don't worry if men don't talk much. For them, not talking is perfectly normal.

Men complain that women talk over them. Brain scans show that women can speak and listen simultaneously. Men can't, so let them finish their sentences.

The threat of, "I'll never talk to you again!" relates to female communication and makes no sense to a man.

Talk to men in direct
terms and say exactly
want you mean. Don't
beat around the bush.

Tell a man whether you want him to listen or to solve your problems - or all you'll get will be solutions.

The meaning of words is
what men use for power.
That's why they define your
words in an argument.

A woman sees thinking
out loud as being friendly
and sharing. A man feels
pressured and thinks she's
giving him a list of problems
she expects him to fix.

Men were never great conversationalists

Language is not specific
in male brains. Ask a teenage
boy about a party he
attended and he'll mumble,
"Uhh...good." A teenage girl
will give a detailed report of
everything – who said what to
whom, how everyone felt and
what they were wearing.

Don't be anxious when a
man completely shuts off.
He's just gone into
problem-solving mode.

If you are presenting an idea
to a group of men and women,
use male speaking structure
to make your points. Both
sexes can follow man-talk
but men have difficulty
following a woman's
multi-tracked conversations
and can quickly lose interest.

Men use direct speech
and take words literally.

When a man is speaking, do not feed back his emotions - just sit there expressionless, nod, grunt and don't interrupt.

When you verbalise a series of items out loud in random order, listing all the options and possibilities, men become confused. Keep it simple!

The compartmentalised
male brain becomes broken
down by alcohol. That's why
drunk men phone at 2am
and won't stop talking.

Because males can only do
one thing at a time,
women say, "Look at me
when I speak to you."

Women use silence to punish men. But men like silence.

Men take turns in talking. When a man is having his turn, let him have it. Don't interrupt.

A man sees excessive
talking as an interference
in his problem-solving
process and prefers to sit
on his rock and fire-gaze.

~ Spatial Awareness ~

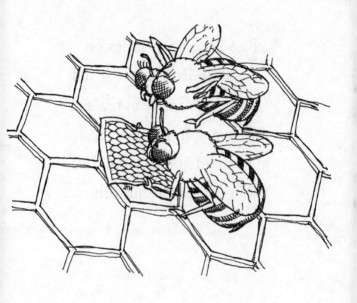

"For the fifth time Nathan ...
stop and ask for directions!"

Reading maps relies on spatial ability. Brain scans show it's strong in males but weak in females. If a man hands you a map, tell him to read it himself.

Why did Moses spend 40 years wandering in the desert? He refused to ask for directions.

Most men can point
north - most women can't.
Ask a man to give you
directions involving
landmarks such as
'Drive past McDonald's
and head for the building
with the National
Bank sign on top.'

A male brain sees an architectural plan of a house three-dimensionally. Men can see how a plan drawing would look as a finished house.

When the requirement for the job is pure spatial ability and mathematical reasoning, men still dominate. This is why 91% of actuaries, 99% of all engineers and 98% of cockpit crews are male.

Boys love their toys – this is why 99% of all patents are registered by men.

Don't let a man force you to park the car. Estimating the distance between the car bumper and the garage wall while moving is a spatial skill which is not strong in most women.

If a man is driving in the car alone, he'll stop and ask for directions. But to do so in front of a woman is to fail.

Men love impractical,
spatially-related toys.
If it beeps, blinks and
needs at least six D-cell
batteries, most men want one.

~ Perceptions ~

"HELP!
We are lost, but our dad
won't stop to ask for directions!"

Strive for equality.

Get your own remote control.

Men consider a woman with a deeper voice more intelligent, authoritative and credible. You can practise this.

When you try on a new
dress and ask, "How does it
look?", a man thinks it's a
problem-solving question.

It's not that men
are insensitive. Their brains
just aren't organised to
notice small details and
changes in the appearance
or behaviour of others.

When a man doesn't talk,
it's not a cue for believing
something is wrong.

Teach a man that the most valuable thing he can do is to listen and not offer solutions.

To try to gain authority, many women raise their voice. But men think they are aggressive.

To impress men in
business, keep your thoughts
inside your head and only
talk about conclusions.

Men don't show emotion when they listen. Women who also listen with a 'poker face' are rated by men as more believable and rational.

When a man is thinking,
he looks like he's bored or idle.
Don't talk to him or give
him things to do.

Men become angry when interrupted because they can't concentrate on more than one thing at a time.

Men often enjoy a quiet drink after work. And that's exactly what it is – quiet.

A man's self-worth is
measured by your
appreciation for his efforts.

To prove his love for her,
he climbed the highest
mountain, swam the
deepest ocean and crossed
the widest desert. But she
left him – he was never home.

Don't offer a man advice
unless he asks for it – tell him
you have confidence in his
ability to work things out.

How many men does it take to change a toilet roll? No one knows. It's never happened.

In a man's heaven, he has three remote controls and toilet seats are left up.

If you are a woman working in
a traditional male hierarchy,
you now have one of two
choices: quit or masculinize.

~ Sex, Love & Romance ~

Waiting for Mr Right

How to Satisfy a Woman Every Time:
Caress, praise, pamper, relish, savour,
massage, fix things, empathise, serenade,
compliment, support, feed, soothe,
tantalise, humour, placate, stimulate,
stroke, console, hug, ignore fat bits,
cuddle, excite, pacify, protect, phone,
anticipate, smooch, nuzzle, forgive,
accessorise, entertain, charm, carry for,
oblige, fascinate, attend to, trust, defend,
clothe, brag about, sanctify, acknowledge,
spoil, embrace, die for, dream of, tease,
gratify, squeeze, indulge, idolise, worship.

How to Satisfy a Man Every Time:
Arrive Naked.

Men's brains can separate love from sex. If a man has an affair and says it didn't mean anything, he's probably telling the truth.

People in love have
been shown to have better
health and are much less
likely to contract an illness
than those who are not.

The person who said that the way to a man's heart is through his stomach was aiming too high.

Sex is great for your health. Having an amorous interlude an average of three times every week burns up 35,000 kilojoules, which is equal to running 130 kilometres in a year.

A woman wants lots of sex
with the man she loves.
A man wants lots of sex.

Marriage has its good side.
It teaches you loyalty,
forbearance, tolerance,
self-restraint and other
valuable qualities
you wouldn't need if
you'd stayed single.

Teach him that breasts are
as delicate as testicles.

Men give their penis a name
because they don't want a
stranger making 99% of their
decisions for them.

When it comes to sex,
women need a reason;
men need a place.

"Don't look now, but God's
gift to peacocks just arrived!"

Men think making love
is what a woman does
while he's bonking her.

When a man sees a woman naked he becomes stimulated and aroused. When a woman sees a man naked, she usually bursts into laughter.

Brain scans show that,
during sex, a man is so
intent on what he is
doing he's virtually deaf.

For a man, love is love and
sex is sex and sometimes
they happen together.

Men don't fake orgasm –
no man wants to pull a
face like that on purpose.

Over 90% of affairs are
initiated by men but more than
80% are ended by women.

If a woman wants
an intelligent decision from
a man she's better off to
discuss it after sex, when
his brain is clear.

When a man wants to 'make love', he is still likely to call it 'sex'.

Adam came first –
but men usually do.

For a man, his testosterone is highest at sunrise – just before he sets out for the day's hunting. "I woke up at 6 o'clock one morning and my wife was poking me in the back with a broom handle!", said the husband. When he asked her what she was doing, she said, "You try it for a change!"

"... and then one day, after a biology class, Elliot finally saw what his classmates silently thought - his testosterone level was not normal."

Many men think monogamy is
what furniture is made out of.

"You're a lousy lover!" she said. "How can you tell that in two minutes?" he asked.

Women prefer a deeper bass voice in a man as it's a powerful indicator of high testosterone levels, which means greater virility.

Menopause in men is a predictable event – he buys aviator sunglasses, gets a hair transplant, buys a motorcycle, and wears funny clothes.